D1342339

YOUR SOUL IS A RIVER

Nikita Gill

THOUGHT CATALOG Books

Copyright © 2016 by Nikita Gill. All rights reserved.
Published by Thought Catalog Books, a publishing house
based in Williamsburg, Brooklyn and owned by
The Thought & Expression Company (www.thought.is).
This book was produced by Chris Lavergne. Art direction
was led by Mark Kupasrimonkol and project management
was handled by Alex Zulauf. Illustrations are by Amanda
Mocci. The digital version was built by KJ Parish.

For you
who has loved me
in ways
I have never
loved myself.

THE COSMOS
1

FIRE
2

THE STORM
3

ACHE
4

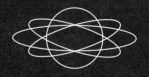

1
—

THE
COSMOS

What a perfect collision of stars it was
that came together at just the right moment
at just the right time,
to build the incredible thing that is you.

I

"What if I told you
for this moment between us,
the whole universe
had to be created?"

II

"And what if I told you
that every part of you comes
from every star you ever saw
in the night sky?"

YOU MATTER

You are not small.
You are not unworthy.
You are not insignificant.
The universe wove you from a constellation
just so, every atom, every fibre in you
comes from a different star.

Together,
you are bound by stardust,
altogether spectacularly created
from the energy of the universe itself.

And that, my darling,
is the poetry of physics,
the poetry of you.

DO NOT FEAR THE DARK

As a child, I used to be afraid of the dark
until you drew open the curtains
and showed me the stars.

And sometimes I would forget
and still shiver in fear
and you would remind me gently,

"Do not fear the dark.
Instead, awaken the sleeping wolf inside you
and welcome the night like it is home."

BALANCE

People always want
to be the light
to each other.

Instead aspire to be
each other's darkness
as much as the light.

Be the thing
that helps the other
shine.

Be the thing
that shines
in the dark.

But be these things
to each other
in turn.

YOU ARE THE SUN

The universe did not
breathe star fire into your bones
just so you could burn yourself out
over someone who treats you
like a cigarette break.

You deserve someone who knows
there is stardust in your veins
and that you are the sun.

And the sun does not shine
because someone else wants it to.

It shines because that
is what it was born to do.

COSMIC STORM

Your body was designed to contain a cosmic storm.
It is no wonder that sometimes your head and heart hurt so
much that you may just explode.

It takes a nebula, a cosmic storm of epic proportions
falling apart to create a star.

So be easy on yourself.

You are a storm in transition,
even as these words are being written.

EVOLUTION

Our whole universe is constantly evolving.
Entire stars disappear and new ones take their place.
From the bones of one planet, another is born.
Whole constellations disappear
in the blink of an eye leaving
just stardust in their wake.

What makes you believe
that your soul's journey,
your soul's evolution will
be any less painless?

FEARS

When I was young,
I was afraid of everything.
Spiders, snakes, sharks,
clowns, ghosts,
banshees, werewolves,
aliens, monsters,
the darkness, death,
heartache.

But today, if you asked me
how many things I fear,
I will say just one.
Losing you.

13 BILLION YEAR OLD ATOMS

Still yourself.
Calm. Breathe deeply.
Understand that you are not
nor have ever been alone.

Listen to the way
your heart beats,
and sense the blood
that rushes through your body.

Can you feel them?

The 13 billion year old atoms
that make up the seas
are the same that run through
the bodies of you and me.

Our bodies were made
to house oceans of galaxies,
and our souls are rivers
that have flowed through centuries.

BEAUTIFUL,
TERRIBLE THINGS

You are a thing
both beautiful
and terrible,
and you deserve
someone
who treats you
like the moon
and can love
the dark side
of your soul too.

93 PERCENT STARDUST

We have calcium in our bones,
iron in our veins,
carbon in our souls,
and nitrogen in our brains.
93 percent stardust,
with souls made of flames,
we are all just stars
that have people names.

SILENCE

I have learned to treasure
silence in your departure.
The absence of your footsteps
is no longer how I describe it.

I go to bed alone every night
and I do not grieve
because silence is a sweeter sound
than a heart that doesn't beat for you.

The truth is
I have understood
in your disappearance
in how many ways I can grow.

The epiphany,

Our little planet may be full of sound
but the most powerful stars
in the cosmos were born
in complete silence.

DAMAGED, BROKEN
AND UNHINGED

They see you as damaged and broken and unhinged.
And they tiptoe around you like your feelings are so fragile,
like you do not know how to understand
the difference between kindness and cruelty,
like you are a ticking time bomb
about to go off any second.

And at some point you
started believing it.

At some point you thought
they are right and you are wrong,
you aren't a survivor,
instead you are an unpredictable thing
made of hurt and pain.

Stop.

You are so much more.

You see,
you may be damaged and broken and unhinged.
But so are shooting stars and comets.

LESSONS FROM THE NIGHT SKY

I

They say that the stars twinkle.
Yet this isn't true, because you see,
it is not the stars that twinkle,
but the light they reflect in you and in me.

II

People often talk about reaching for the stars, but it is the stars whose light travels billions of lightyears away to reach us.

III

Never be afraid of asking for help. Even the stars do. Not a single star in the night sky is one, they are binary, which means their light comes from two - two souls shining as one to create each individual tiny light you see before you.

IV

There are two kinds of people who look at the night sky.
Those that look up only to see a graveyard of stars.
And those that look up and see a sea of souls,
shining brightly to guide us home.

Which one are you?

LESSONS FOR WHEN YOU FALL

I

There is something you must know
when you think you have fallen so low,
that all your dreams have turned to dust.

Every star in the sky,
and even the comets that pass by
were made from clouds of floating dust.

II

Don't let the fall fool you
into thinking you are ordinary
when the universe wove you
with the same magic
as the constellations and galaxies.

III

Even shooting stars
must fall
to learn how to soar.

STARS SHINE BRIGHTEST

Sometimes the happiest
and most carefree people
hide the stormiest,
painful ache inside their hearts.

You cannot predict
what is in someone's heart.
Stars always shine brightest
seconds before
they fall apart.

.

ROGUE PLANET

The day you left,
I realised you were a rogue planet.
That you didn't orbit around anyone or anything.

That you had no solar system
and you found your way into mine, into my orbit,
to stay with me for just for a little while.

I couldn't keep you.
You weren't meant
to be a part of me.

Our love was like the sun,
ninety-nine percent of this solar system,
but not nearly enough to keep you.

Some things are more beautiful
because they don't belong
to anyone or anything.

That is how I would like to remember you.
As something too wild for me to keep,
rather than a thing that threw the sun away.

WHAT YOU ARE.
WHAT YOU ARE NOT.

You are:

A walking, breathing universe
of thoughts, ideas, stories as your stars
supernovas full of adventure in your veins
galaxies of emotion.

An untamed, powerful ocean
of every experience that made you
into a journey full of storms
and quiet starry nights.

A sky that has held
the worst of storms
but never forgotten
to let the sun shine through

But you are not and never have been
an apology, a mistake
or a thing to be forgotten.
Remember that in the way
you wear your skin every morning.

IN THIS ROOM

The distance between
the sun and the earth
is 149.6 million km.

The distance between
your heart and mine
is seventeen inches.

Yet somehow,
the sun feels closer to me
in this moment than you.

I STOPPED WISHING ON STARS

I spend nights after you sitting on my window ledge,
studying the stars a little harder than I should,
but not wishing, never wishing on them for you
because now I know those wishes don't come true.

This isn't a movie.

You cannot control other people's lives
with your wishes and destinies are not mapped
in a black velvet sky sprinkled with diamonds,
even if it is the most beautiful thing you have ever seen.

The stars do not bring people back.
No matter how much you miss them or need them.

No one tells you
that hope can sometimes be a dead thing.
Just like no one ever tells you
that you are wishing upon dead stars.

PARENTAL ADVICE

My mother warned me,
that good people are like the stars,
few and far between.

My father reminded me,
that there are so many stars
which I have not yet seen.

A CURE TO FEAR

Place your fears
at the altar
of the night sky.

Feel the moon's glow
on your skin
soft and sweet,
and the still of the air
as you admire
the stars.

Tell me.
Are you still
afraid?

TELL YOUR CHILDREN

Tell your future children
stories about how
you carried them with
more love and care
than if you had
the entire moon
in your womb.

Tell them
how they are
more precious
than any star
even the sun
himself.

THE GIRL IN BLUE

In the Willoughby Cemetery
in a tiny town in Sexton,
there is a small gravestone
that simply reads

'The Girl in Blue.
Killed by Train.
December 24, 1933.
Unknown.
But Not Forgotten.'

Although the loss of a young life is always tragic,
there is something so human but magic
about an entire town coming together
to give a stranger they have never met,
never even known
a peaceful place,
to even in death,
call *her own.*

MYTH FROM A SMALL TOWN

There is a myth
in our sleepy little town
about a girl who climbed
too far up the hill
chasing a shooting star
on a crystal clear night.

She was so
captivated by its beauty,
that she didn't see the car
racing up the forgotten hill road.

They say that her soul was so beautiful
the shooting star collected her bones
and gave them back to the universe
so that it could weave her into a constellation.

The most beautiful thing
about this myth
is how it has made sure,
that everyone remembers
the girl who spent her bones
to make it as pure.

2

—

FIRE

All the darkness of the night
is no match for a single candle
that refuses to die out.

FLAMES YOU LEFT

What else
was I going to do
with all this fire
you left inside me?

I had two choices:
find someone
to share it with,
or to burn alive.

BURNING

Tell me how to to love again
when the ashes of my heart
and smoke in my chest
are evidence that love burns
everything it touches.

The next time love wants to take you,
think of yourself as a forest.
When a wildfire comes to devastate you
instead of just surviving it,
you learned to grow in ashes.

THREE THINGS

There are only three things
you have ever showed me.

How to start a fire,
how easy it is to set alight
someone who loves you,
and how to stand back, watching,
doing nothing as they burn.

Now let me show you how
I let your flames destroy me,
how I built myself up from the ashes,
and how people who are half phoenix
can resurrect when burned.

QUESTIONS ABOUT
A LOVE THAT WAS

Questions I wanted to ask you
when we were ending
but didn't.

I

How does something that set fire
to your heart
suddenly chill your bones?

II

How does a thing
that was once so warm,
grow so very cold?

III

How do you go back
to being strangers
with someone who has seen your soul?

I

A day will come
when you will look at yourself
in the mirror and marvel at
how wonderful it is,
how exquisite it is,
to be completely devoid
of the sadness
of the loneliness
that once clung to your skin
like salt to an open wound.

You have grown so much
because you have quietly realised
you aren't just teardrops.
You are an ocean.

II

You found yourself
in a battlecry of blood
in fires of war
in breaking skin.

Consider for a moment
for a second
how incredibly resilient
your spirit is.

III

No one teaches us
how to recover
when we are burned by love.

No one shows us
how to touch someone
without burning them
with the flames of those
we once loved.

Nobody tells us
the secret to stop
tasting like ashes.
Or how to stop setting fire
to those who love us.

That is the thing
about old flames.
They may die out
but the embers burn
never leaving us the same.

DARK AND LIGHT

And then,
she reminded me
"There may be darkness
within this world.
But inside us the light burns
brighter than you
could ever know."

FAVOURITE

When they ask you
who your first love was,
don't breathe his name,
don't whisper hers.

When they ask you
who healed your heart,
don't attribute it to him
don't credit her.

When they ask you
for your favourite poem,
don't say it was him,
don't say it was her.

Say it is you.
Always.
It is *you*.

FLAMMABLE

Of all the things
that are most flammable
in the history of the world,
I have encountered
nothing
more flammable
than the human heart.

FOREST SET AFLAME

You were a forest,
your lungs filled with
butterflies and magic,
your heart a hidden lake
and the souls of
a thousand ancient trees
resting beneath your skin.
And then, one day,
someone came along
on a windy day.
And lit the match
that started
a devastating fire.

I LOOK AT YOU AND WONDER

I look at you and sometimes wonder:
How can a broken thing be so pretty?
Can the whole sun be captured in a human body?
Can darkness become one with light?
Would the universe allow a star to burn this bright?
Does the earth have it in itself to hold this much beauty?

And whilst looking at you, I learn:
You are living proof that fire can rise again
even from cold ashes.

FIRE IS NOT A TOY

As a child they tell you to stay away from the flames.
"Fire is not a toy," they insist, wrenching the box from
your hands before you burn your fingertips.

They think they are protecting you,
but they never ask why you were playing
with matches in the first place.

They took those matches to protect you.
But who is going to protect you
from the darkness
that lives inside of you?

And in a way,
even as a child
you envy
how the flames
never have to apologise
for hurting
anyone.

FIRE AND ASH

I

This is the way you chose to love me:

Like flames ripping through a forest,
like fire corroding the last of it.
Like the ashes that remain.

II

This is the way I chose to love you:

I already knew
what you were going to do.

III

Some people will always taste like fire
and leave the ones that love them
tasting like ash.

3
—

THE
STORM

A hurricane never apologises
for the chaos it leaves in its wake.

THE SECRET INSIDE ME

I have wrapped my heart
in iron, and chained it
to my rib cage;
not to stop you
from getting in,
but to stop
the hurricanes
of pain,
of memories,
of destruction,
from getting out.

IF THEY TRULY LOVE YOU

If they truly love you,
they will love you
when you are an ocean breeze,
but also when you are a summer storm.

You were not made
to be loved in parts,
you were meant
to be loved
as a whole.

LET GO

For even the ocean
must let go of the hurricane
in the end,
though she knows
she will never
see him again.

HANDLE THIS

I thought you said
you could handle a storm
that you could calm a tornado,
that you spoke chaos
like it was your mothertongue.

I thought this meant
you understood the whirlwind,
you could withstand heavy rainfall,
and you knew how to bear down
against the winds of a hurricane.

Turns out,
you saw a little drizzle
as chaos and ran
when you realised that
my mind was torrential rain.

PERSPECTIVES

Some people are born with
tornados in their lives,
but constellations in their eyes.
Other people are born
with stars at their feet,
but their souls are lost at sea.

STORM BRINGERS

Prelude

Some people are chaos
from the moment
they walk into your life
to the second they leave it.

The Calm Before

And when you meet him,
you will realise
that sometimes
they make people
who have tornados
instead of souls.

The Aftermath

You fell in love with a storm.
Did you really think
you would get out
unscathed?

The Calm Before

Girls like her were born in a storm.
they have lightning in their souls,
Thunder in their hearts,
and chaos in their bones.

The Aftermath

But you didn't fall in love
with a person.
You fell in love
with a hurricane
that had grown
a beating heart and skin.

LESSONS FROM THE WIND

After you left,

She took her lessons

From the wind.

You knew her as an ocean breeze.

Now,

Know her as a hurricane.

THE EYE OF THE STORM

I

I thought I was safe
in the eye of your storm
but then,
without warning
you blinked,
and I was gone.

II

I suppose I have
only myself to blame.
I knew
you were going to destroy me
but I refused
to get out of your way.

CONTROL

I

Your heart and the weather
have this in common.
They are both difficult to predict,
and cannot be controlled by anyone.

So when someone tries
to take control of what is yours,
remind them that
storms are controlled by no one,
and then show them
how you are
so much more
than a storm.

II

You carry both lightning and thunder
in that space between your bones and soul.
Become the storm you are hiding from;
a hurricane does not run from the rain.

HURRICANES ARE THIEVES

You have always reminded me of a hurricane.

But not because you are beautiful,
or a force of nature,
but because hurricanes are thieves.

They breathe in at the ocean's surface,
drawing from her life force,
taking from her soul,
before disappearing into oblivion
to cause destruction, devastation.

And just like you, they never ever return.

SELF DESTRUCT

You were a mess before
any of this happened.
Insecure and afraid
and more than a little broken.

One day someone said
you reminded them of a storm.

And you believed them, didn't you?
Spun a little faster like a hurricane
saved your body for the wind
for the day it would take you away.

Did you forget
what you understood as a child
that storms outlive butterflies
by a few mere days?

Now here you are
in your own aftermath.
Tell me is today the day
you finally learn to love yourself?

PASSING STORM

Last night,
the windows rattled
the floors shook
the rain nearly broke
every single window
inside my house.

I stood there
watching,
learning,
understanding
as the storm passed
how even destructive things
like our love
were not built
to last forever.

FLOODS

Why have you
flooded
all four chambers
of your heart
with such love
for people
who are not
worthy
of you?

INTO THE WIND

When you leave your words
to carelessly scatter
in the wind,
you do not know
where they will go,
who will recieve them
and what consequence
they will have.

WORLD'S END

This world has gone dark
more times than you
or your mother
or her mother
can remember.
And every hurricane
that was meant to be
the end of it all
has instead ended
in sunshine
again.

So believe me
when I say:
You will survive this.
And the next one too.

4
—
ACHE

These aren't scars.

These are stories.

A LIST OF THINGS
TO COME TO TERMS WITH

I

When someone decides the way you grieve, it is time to let
them go. Your tears weren't designed with a stopclock in
mind, you are allowed to drain the ocean of them if need be.
Do not allow them to be shamed into a painful,
numbing silence.

II

If he tells you that the change in you has left you a shell of
the person he once loved, remind him how he once called
you a wildflower and how he always said that some people
see them as flowers and others as weeds. Ask him when he
became the latter.

III

If you hate the sun for shining on the day you lose the
warmest things you have ever loved, remember how even
the earth will lose the warmth of the sun one day, but
unlike you, will not survive the loss.

IV

The last time you kiss someone
does not have to feel like
you are losing them
in a war.

V

If they walk out a door that you opened,
you are still allowed to grieve
for the life you lost with them.
But whatever you do,
never forget why you opened it
in the first place.
And never forget to close that door,
once they have walked out.

VI

Some loves do not have the right soil for roses to grow.

VII

Even you have not been permanent to people.

FOUR POEMS ABOUT CHAOS

I

Before I dreamed of chaos,
now I dream of you.

I don't know which is more terrifying
losing my own chaos,
or loving you.

II

She was the kind of girl
who was a chaos of contradictions
from one second to the next,
for her mind was never free.
Sometimes bright like the sun,
sometimes calm like the moon,
sometimes stormy like the ocean,
and sometimes all three.

III

Some people survive chaos
and that is how they grow.
And some people thrive in chaos,
because chaos is all they know.

IV

The skin she wears may be made of calm,
but her bones are made out of chaos.

THE ROOM

We all have a room within us,
in which we keep the things
we have loved
deeply,
intensely,
passionately,
but lost forever.

My room is full of you.
Just you.

GRIEF

This is how your grief will look at you:

In the seconds after it happens, you feel the world turning
on its head and you're still standing upright, face forwards,
when everything seems to have reversed and slowed down.
Your mind insists that you have not changed, the world has.
Your heart insists that the world doesn't exist, only you do.
Both are trying to convince you, that you have not become
forlorn, the world is just broken. But your mind is lying
and so is your heart.

Four days after you have picked yourself up from the floor
where you have been since it happened, your mother has
already visited twice and said, "Listen, things will get better.
You just have to let them," and "We can help you," and
"Please." Words seem hollow, but you feel more hollow
than any words, hearing the way they echo and disappear
inside you.

A week after you have forgotten to sleep, forgotten to dream,
forgotten how to communicate in the way those around
you still can. You wonder what breathing without your
heart breaking looks like. You wonder what words without
the taste of death feel like. You wonder what the universe is
trying to tell you through all this. But you never ever wonder
if things get better. Because you are sure they never do.

A month slowly trickles away, the way water does when it is collecting in a bucket from a dripping ceiling. You're still here. This surprises you more than anything else. Because if you are still here, then you are still breathing, despite your best efforts to will your soul away from this broken body.

It's been three months and people have sounded like a stuck record about this for so long, everything is now on autopilot. Get up, shower, get to work, forget to eat, work some more, come home, sometimes remember to eat, go to bed. The routine is numb, but then again, that is why it is comfortable.

The thing with numbness is, it gets into your skin, travels down your veins and into your heart.

The thing with grief is,
it never completely goes away,
no matter how numb you are.

A PROMISE

When you love someone,
promise me you will not love them
like they are a war
and you are the thing
that will help them win.

Promise me,
you will not hunt down
their flaws like enemies
in a battlefield
to kill them.

People were
not made
to be saved
by you
or anyone else.

All we can hope for
in this life
is a chance
to be able
to save ourselves.

5
—

THE SEA, THE RIVER, THE OCEAN

I have learned to fear the water

as much as love her

for she is in every corner

in every essence of me.

FROM THE RIVER BANKS

I

The river has taught me
more about my soul
than any person
I have ever known.

How to adapt to any vessel
How to dream in fluid motion
How to love and then to let go.

II

I have never heard
the river apologise
for taking something
that didn't belong to her.

I have never heard
the river pray
for anything she has ever
wanted or desired.

I have never heard
the river cry
or feel sorry for herself
when things don't go her way.

The river
takes what she wants,
does what she desires
and washes over anything
that stands in her way.

DROWNING

The thing is,
you can't save people
from themselves
because they will
just grab hold of you
like you are a lifeline,
you will both
go under
and neither of you
will emerge.

There is only one way
to save someone
from drowning
and that is
to teach them
how to swim.

A TSUNAMI OF YOU

This love for you
has turned
into a tidal wave
of emotions,
a tsunami
of feelings,
that my body
is not equipped
to swim through.

Do not help me.
For I am drowning
in an ocean
made of you.

UNREQUITED

He is the kind of exquisite
that illuminates lifetimes.
I am the kind of grotesque
that destroys what is divine.
How can someone like him
love something like me
When all I am is a shipwreck
in his deep, blue sea.

THE OCEAN'S BEST KEPT SECRET

When little girls lose their innocence,
and little boys are taught to forget their childhoods,
that is when the world has no hope left.

Preserve innocence.
Preserve childhood.
Even the ocean knows better than us
how to hide its most precious creatures.
That is why 95 percent of the water
despite all our technology
is unknown to us.

ICARUS WARNING

Some things are beautiful,
but they are beautiful in the way
of the sun.
If you fly too close,
they will melt your wings
and send you plummeting
into the sea.

ALL OR NOTHING

She is so passionate,
that sometimes
it scares you.

But you knew this
when you fell
in love with her.

She is the sea.

She loves in floods,
with the intensity
of ten tempests.

Or not at all.

OCEAN PEOPLE

Some people grow entire oceans
inside themselves instead of hearts.

It's why they have more love to
give than anyone can ever return.

It's why they awaken sometimes
to heartache and tear soaked pillows.

Sometimes it is a blessing to love something
so much more than you love yourself.

Sometimes it is a curse to love anything
so much more than you love yourself.

WHEN WE FIGHT

I have lived this story
so many times
and in it
you are always the sea
and I am learning
how to sail your
turbulent waters
but each time I manage
to steady myself
in your current,
you create a tidal wave
that shatters my little sailboat
and I sink into your depths.

THE MOON AND THE SEA

The moon has always been
the ocean's most jealous lover.
But every time he has tried
to fully control her tides,
she has turned into
a terrible tempest
and broken through his chains
with such fury,
only allowing him
the illusion of control
on her smallest, weakest tides.

Remember that you are the ocean.
And no one, not even the moon itself
is allowed to control
your glorious, beautiful tides.

DROWNING SOUL

All these pieces
you have cut out
of your soul to
give to those you say
need them more
than you.

Have you forgotten
how it felt
when you were
drowning
with nothing
to hold onto?

SALT ROSES

The ocean
is full of salt water
no human can drink.

And the last time
we met there, darling
you applied salt water
to every wound
you left inside me,
and planted
salt roses
to grow
in my lungs.

A FINAL LESSON
FROM THE OCEAN

The ocean holds magic
for those who seek it.
But she only bestows
her best magic
on those
who deserve it.

There is a lesson
in that for you.
Give your best
to those who deserve it,
not to everyone
who seeks it.

4
—

WILD

If you love a wild thing,
have the courage to leave it
as wild as you found it.

ON YOUR INNER WILD

If they cannot understand
the wildness inside you,
they will try to tame it
and cage it.
Find someone who appreciates
the beauty of wild things
like you.

YOU ARE A FRIGHTENINGLY
BEAUTIFUL WILD THING

There are boys
who are going to promise you
forevers in song,
in poetry,
in words that are just so damned pretty
they will be hard to resist.

You're their dream girl.
Beautiful, strong, independent.
Forever, they sigh, forever.

But their forevers come
with hidden terms and conditions, their love
is a secret contract,
with addendums and asterisks.

Forever is only
until you start dreaming too much, talking too loudly,
kissing too strongly,
and debating too heatedly.

It's not girl-like, they will say,

you're hard to understand, they will rationalise,
impossible for anyone to put up with
let alone love.

Can't you be beautiful in limitation?
Strong sometimes but weak more often?
Independent whilst being helpless?
They will ask you to be
all these impractical things
without thinking that these
are all the same qualities
they once fell in love with.

They are going to make you doubt yourself, beautiful.
And even then, even when they have wronged you,
misunderstood your debates for insolence
misinterpreted your strength for arrogance,
you will reach inside yourself
to find the things they are looking for,
because you want – you need to be loved.

You will learn to talk quietly,
love gingerly,
dream a little less,
let him kiss you instead.

Stop.

You do not need to change yourself,
for boys who fell in love with
a beautiful, wild thing
that they are too ill equipped
and must cage to 'handle'.

You do not make yourself less
when you are a comet filled with such power and intensity,
that you are
waiting to blaze
across this universe.

You are unexplored, unusual
and frighteningly beautiful.
And only a few will understand
the way to love you
without breaking you
and making you dangerous.

THE NEXT TIME

And when they try to force
something you love away
from you again,
you have a decision to make.

Are you just going
to let them take from you
silently like a sheep?

Or are you
going to channel
everything wild within you,
and fight them
like a wolf?

PRIMAL

Love is a deeply primal thing
when you give your heart to someone
when you let them into your mind
when you feel them in your veins.

Love is a deeply primal thing
we match it with red, as red as blood
because everything we love
is marked with our bloodstains.

MOTHER

Your mother never gave up her wild.
You can still see it in her eyes
when something makes her ache.
The way a wolf's eyes gleam
with ferocity
when she senses
her young is in danger.

YOUR LOVE

Your love was born in the wild,
growing from the soft earth
surrounded by trees
that were surrounded by stars.

That is why the forest
has such a hold on you.
That is why sometimes it feels
like the moon knows your name.

SOFT

You say my love
is soft and gentle,
and soft things have
always been harmless.

You are right.
My love is soft.

Like a gentle stag
protecting his family
from hunters.

Like the soft fur of a fox
quietly watching
for prey.

Who told you
that soft things
were never
dangerous?

THE VESSEL

Remember that your body is a vessel
for the wild, extraordinary thing
that lives inside you.

Allow your pain be finite.
Wild things bear no grudges
when they are set free.

THE DAY YOU LEFT

The most important lesson
I learnt on the day
you left me
is the realisation
nothing that is truly wild
ever weeps for its broken heart.

THE DRAWING

He drew her once.
Too pretty, too perfect,
like she was a work of art
and she hated her
- that beautiful girl he drew,
because her flaws are her journey.

Her slightly misaligned jaw
from ill fated punch,
her long battle with scars,
her nose that was
always a bit too big for her face.

Perhaps he sees her as flawless.

But she,
like a wild thing
which has been injured
but survived the hunt,
was more beautiful
with all her damage intact.

7
—

THE
EARTH

Imagine how much more you would feel for her,
if you knew that the earth had a heartbeat.

MOTHER EARTH

The earth grew you
limb by limb
within her womb.

You owe it to her
not to turn her body
into a tomb.

EARTH TRUTHS

Some days you will break
every part of yourself
until there is nothing left
that you truly know.

Do not blame yourself
when this happens.
Even the earth breaks
to allow flowers to grow.

WHEN THEY LEAVE

When someone plants flowers
in parts of your spirit
that were dark
closed,
broken
before they arrived,
do not let them wither
when they leave.

Instead,
love them for growing
love them for living
love them for letting the light
back into your soul.

SPIRIT

My spirit was
a thousand sleeping birds
hiding inside
a deep, dark forest
until you arrived
and awakened them all
inside of me.

HOPING

I hope you fall in love with someone
well versed in the language
of forests and monsoon.

I hope you fall in love with someone
who loves you like the wolf
loves the moon.

THE EARTH AND THE OCEAN

I wonder if the earth
ever heard the ocean
cry for the people she lost
when they drowned
inside her depths.

WHEN IT FEELS LIKE THE END

My darling,
I know it seems like the end of the world,
that everything has been destroyed,
that the whole earth is in flames.

But remember,
there are beginnings in endings,
through destruction there comes life
and you have the same strength in you
that makes the phoenix rise
from the flames.

HUMAN SHAPED LIBRARIES

If every single one of
your beautiful, terrible emotions
could be translated into words,
even the biggest library on earth
would not be able to handle
the amount of books you could write.

8
—
HEAL

Let it hurt.
Let it bleed.
Let it heal.
And let it go.

YOUR HEART AND SKIN

Your heart is not a hotel
with rooms to rent out
whenever you find yourself
alone.

Turn your alone
into a place of comfort.
Your skin should be
a place that you can call home.

HEALING FROM ABUSE

People forget
that abuse
is damaging,
but its aftermath
is permanent.

Your body will heal,
and so will your mind
but when things heal
they leave scars
behind.

You owe no one
an explanation,
a reason,
a defence
for who you become
after you survive.

THIS STRANGE AGE

I am
young enough
to remember
how to love
without boundaries
but
old enough
to know
how to be cautious
with what I allow
into my soul.

FOUR LESSONS
I LEARNED ABOUT LOVE

I

In the beginning,
there was darkness...
...and then love was born.

II

I have two hearts.
One that you took with you
and one which I had to grow anew.

III

Here are your choices in both love and war.
You either come back forever changed,
or you do not come back at all.

IV

You have turned your heart
into a museum of people
you've loved to keep them alive inside you.

WARS INSIDE YOU

There are silences inside you
that you have yet to explore.
There are things inside you
that are still fighting a war.

Some days will be unkind
Some days you will want to forget
But stay for those days
that are worth more than all the rest.

Be easy on your soul
it needs softness
it needs time
it needs patience.

STAY

Be careful
when you ask
love to stay.

Not every love
is kind
and true.

But every love
leaves fingerprints
on your heart forever.

YOUR NAME

One day you will awaken
and your own name
will no longer taste like pain,
Your body will not burn
with fingerprints
that don't belong there.
Your mind will no longer
bleed with memories
that make you unholy to yourself.
And that is when
you know
you are finally
returning home to yourself.

YOUR LONELY CALLS TO ME

Your lonely
is so lovely.

It makes me wonder
how something
so beautiful
can be so very sad.

YOU

And first,
before him
and before her
and before them
there was *you*.

Never forget that.

LESSONS FROM THE RAIN

The next time you cry,
take a lesson from the rain.
Learn the way
she never holds back her storm
or how loud her tears are
when they fall.

A MIDNIGHT THOUGHT

I hope you find someone
who knows how to love you
when you are sad.

NATURAL LESSONS

The sky is never the same shade twice
and neither is your heart.

The moon has never apologised
for hiding some nights
and neither should you.

The stars have never stopped shining
because someone wanted them to
and neither should you.

The earth has never stopped
moving,
growing,
evolving
for *anyone*
and *neither should you.*

GUILT

You have survived,
but you have hurt others to do so
and that is a terrible burden
to carry.

When you grow this guilt
locked in a chest
in the attic of your heart,
consider this:
there are a million ways to say
I love you,
but only a few honest ways
to apologise.

You do not belong to the monster
that hides inside your chest.
It belongs to you
and you belong to yourself.

Apologise.

And give your tired heart respite.

THE CHILD INSIDE

The way you hate yourself
sometimes,
you seem to forget
that there is still a child
somewhere inside you,
and you're feeding
that innocence
within you
poison
with those
cruel words.

Protect that child
by being gentler
with yourself.

Protect that child
by being kinder
by yourself.

Because no one else
will protect them
other than you.

THIS BRUISED SKIN

I

To be fully human
fully kind and true
is full of bruising.

Because
that is how things
become soft.

II

What you have
hidden inside
your skin.

It is more precious
than diamonds
or gold.

SILENCED

They only succeed
in stealing your voice
if you give them
permission
by silencing yourself.

BECOMING

Become the person
you wished
your parents
your friends
your siblings
were when you
needed them
the most.

DISAPPEARANCE

When you disappear
into a haze
of love soaked promise,
remember the person
you were before
those promises were made.

Don't allow that person
to disappear too.

BELIEVE YOU CAN

You must plunge
heart first
if you want
to test your wings.

PAINFUL TRUTHS

The painful truths we choose
not to acknowledge
about ourselves
become our
biggest
regrets

BE KIND

Be kind.

There is strength
in kindness.

For it is only when
a kind person
starts to grow
thorns
you realise
how strong
their heart really is.

STORM CHILD, I LOVE YOU

I do not want to love you
in fair weather.

It is easy to love
a sunny day
where the breeze
is cool on your back
as the sun beats down
hard on you.

No.

I want you to give me
your storm,
tornados of emotions
the parts of you
that hide away
because no one else
can handle them.

Storms
apologise to no one,
my darling,

and neither
should you.

So let it out,
let it all out,
and let me show you
that you are
as easy to love
in passion,
as you are
in serenity.

DETERMINED

When you use words like
I can't, I won't
It isn't possible
I am incapable,
Remember this.

Your spine is stronger
than granite.
You have no reason
to act like
it doesn't exist.

PAIN

Pain speaks one language.
You owe it to yourself
not to become fluent
in it.

THE SOUND OF HEARTBREAK

It is eerily terrifying that there is no sound when a heart breaks. Car accidents end with a bang, falling ends with a thud, even writing makes the scratching sound of pencil against paper. But the sound of a heart breaking is completely silent. Almost as though no one, not even the universe itself could create a sound for such devastation. Almost as though silence is the only way the universe could pay its respect to the sound of a heart falling apart.

PANIC ROOM

In my head,
there is a place
where all the people
who once loved you
who were once loved
by you
still live.

And it is not
a place of pain.
It is a place
where you keep the things
that promised to stay
with you forever...

But never did.

YOUR LOVE

The way you have loved
speaks volumes about you.

The way they leave speaks
volumes about them.

Your love is not poison.
Their inability to appreciate it *is*.

LONELINESS

When every part of you
aches with loneliness,
seek no one else.

Now is the time
to seek yourself.

SOUL SONGS

I

The most beautiful souls
weren't woven
from silk, seamless
and untouched
by human fingers.

They are weathered from age,
worn by time,
and patched time and time
again by loving hands.

II

Show me
the most damaged
parts of your soul,
and I will show you
how it still shines
like gold.

III

You are a dangerous collection
of all my favourite things.

An old soul,
a heart of gold
and hands that
make my body
sing.

THE ASPEN GROVE

In the Wasatch Mountains in Utah,
there is an Aspen Grove
made of 47,000 trees.

Until they discovered
that it was not
a forest of trees
but one single organism,
joined together
by a single root system
connected
so strongly,
so intimately
that it forms
an entire forest,
tough,
breathing,
beautiful,
and the largest organism
in the world.

Your broken heart
is like this Aspen Grove.
It may feel broken right now,
and on the surface,
a few trees,
a few pieces of you
may be missing.
But underneath the ground
there are a thousand strong roots
keeping it strong,
keeping it beating
and *keeping you alive.*

TOUGH

You don't have to prove to anyone just how tough you are.
You are still here, and you are still alive despite all of life's
storms and tornados and hurricanes.

You have weathered them all like a grand old oak tree, and
you are still here.

You are still alive.

And if that isn't tough, I don't know what is.

NEW BEGINNINGS

I

Everything dead
everything forgotten
everything buried
coming alive again.
That is the magic
of Spring
and your spirit.

II

Every morning
the sun rises and you,
like the plants
covered in dew
in your garden
get a chance
to start again.

Good morning.
Your world fell apart
yesterday.

And yet,
here is your second chance
to rebuild it.

III

In Sanskrit,
one of the world's
most ancient languages,
one does not not say
'Good morning'.

Instead,
one says
'Shubh arambh',
which translated means
'good beginnings'.

So to you I say
Shubh arambh
May you have
a thousand
good beginnings.

WITH
DEEPEST
GRATITUDE
TO

My parents and grandparents for letting me write to my heart's content and giving me the gift of stories.

My brother for being himself.

My South African family for planting more stories to grow in my heart.

The One for reminding me to be myself when even I had forgotten who that was.

Chris and Mélanie for seeing the universe I created in my mind and believing in it, and in me.

My iPresent family for being the warmth and fun and joy I needed all along.

Mary for seeing the magic always.

Clare for being my big sister when I needed one the most.

Tree for reminding me what powerful things words can be.

And all of you, who have joined me on this incredible journey. I hope you find what you are looking for.

ABOUT THE PUBLISHER

Thought Catalog Books is a publishing house owned by
The Thought & Expression Company, an independent
media group based in Brooklyn, NY. Founded in 2010,
we are committed to facilitating thought and expression.
We exist to help people become better communicators and
listeners in order to engender a more exciting, attentive,
and imaginative world.

Visit us on the web at *www.thought.is* or
www.thoughtcatalog.com.

ABOUT THE WRITER

Nikita Gill lives just outside a forest in England. She's a
writer, photographer, and graphic designer. She loves the
night sky.

Find her on *facebook.com/nikitagillwrites* or
instagram.com/nikita_gill.